Book 3 of the Decency Journey series

COPING IN A TOXIC ENVIRONMENT

Anna Eliatamby

ISBN: 978-1-80443-011-8

British Library Cataloguing in Publication Data.
A catalogue record for this book is available from the British Library.

This pocketbook also contains some concepts from
*Healthy Leadership and Organisations: Beyond the
Shadow Side.* Anna Eliatamby (Editor).2022.

PREFACE

This pocketbook is part of a series on healthy leadership and organisations for decency. The aim is to encourage you to look at what is golden and shadow in your work as leaders and as organisations, so people can detox and heal. When we focus on the golden, and address the shadow, then we are more likely to be decent in all we say and do.

Decency is 'honest, polite behaviour that follows accepted moral standards and shows respect for others' (Oxford Learners Dictionary).

We all contribute to what is golden (positive) and shadow (negative) in work and life. Mostly we operate from the golden side, but sometimes we function from the shadow side, and this holds us back as individuals and as organisations. We are all human and fallible.

Let's give ourselves permission to explore the positive and negative so that we create a better balance between the golden and shadow for ourselves and the wider world community. This way, we can contribute to a healthier world both for us now and for the generations to come. And we may yet achieve better decency for us all.

The titles in the Decency Journey Series are:

Healthy Leadership
Healthy Organisations
Coping In A Toxic Environment
Your Own Toxic Work Behaviours
Building an Organisational Mental Health and Well-being Strategy
Volcanoes, Personal Healing and Change
Our Journey for Diversity and Inclusion in Business

CONTENTS

OUR APPROACH

This pocketbook is based on a model that we describe in our book *Healthy Leadership and Organisations: Beyond the Shadow Side*. Here are the key elements that we use as a basis for this pocketbook.

WHAT IS OVERALL HEALTHINESS?

The words 'healthy' and 'healthiness' refer to physical health and, sometimes, mental health and well-being. All these facets are important components for overall healthiness, but we suggest that there are others. These include synergy between purpose, values, and how we live and work; the impact of material resources and the environment, being willing to be open and listen to the incoming future, and how we live and cope with the shadow side.

All these factors, for overall healthiness, need to be coordinated with compassion and respect by our individual or organisational sense of Self. Collective responsibility for promoting the positive and addressing the negative should be present.

The golden refers to the positive parts of us (kindness, integrity) and of organisations (compassion, working with purpose). The shadow includes dishonesty, bullying, and harassment for individuals and organisations.

Healthiness is an essential ingredient for decency. Without it, we are likely to be unsuccessful.

WHAT IS HEALTHY LEADERSHIP?

Leadership is an individual and collective function that has many intentions. This usually includes an aim to serve human beings and/or something else. Some people operationalize leadership ethically and positively to serve others. Others will have another focus, such as a profit motive, alongside wanting to be ethical.

Healthy leadership happens when the individual or the group do their utmost to serve others ethically and respectfully, while acknowledging that there can be negativity and being willing to address it and heal. They remain flexible and open to sensing the incoming future.

Being and growing as a healthy leader ensures decency in yourself and in how you act at work.

WHAT IS A HEALTHY ORGANISATION?

Why do organisations exist? To enact a greater purpose, sometimes forgotten as the organisation becomes bigger and veers from the intended path.

A healthy organisation ensures it remains true to its purpose, and does no harm to humans or the planet. <u>Do no harm</u>. The organisation always endeavours to provide a nourishing culture and structure within which people can grow and flourish in their work to achieve that purpose. A healthy organisation works to recognise and address unhealthy elements, is amenable to change, and will consider possible futures while operating in the present.

Decency is seen as a core essential and its use flows naturally throughout the organization. People do not have to think about the need to be decent, they just are. Thus, the organization contributes to the greater decency we need for the world.

INTRODUCTION

No one wants to work in a toxic environment, and yet it happens. We rarely notice awfulness at the beginning of our employment. Awareness creeps in until we acknowledge it, and then we try to cope with it.

The psychological impact of working in toxicity is massive. It demotivates us and can significantly add to our vulnerability to problems, such as anxiety and depression. It can prevent us from fully utilising our skills and talents. And trust levels are commonly low.

If we are being targeted by an individual or a group, then we may feel isolated and less inclined to go to work. At its worst, toxicity can also negatively affect our personal lives.

Ideally, such negative work environments should be successfully tackled the instant that people realize the awfulness. But these cultures often continue endlessly, with no meaningful attempts to tackle them. A very few will be brave enough to speak up, hoping to get the issue highlighted and resolved. But most of us endure as best we can; this can take as much strength as whistleblowing.

This pocketbook helps you to learn about the toxic behaviours you may experience and the reasons for their existence. We support you to analyse your current approach and then work out what more you could do to manage in your circumstances.

Throughout this book, please keep remembering how wonderful you are. What is happening to you has nothing to do with you or your sterling (core) qualities. It is simply that others, for reasons best known to themselves, have targeted you. The only 'fault' that you have is the fact that you are breathing–not at all a reason!

THE BEHAVIOURS AND THEIR IMPACT

Toxicity and toxic people can make you feel confused, drained, doubtful, and guilty. You may notice they ignore social boundaries, and more.

Here is a list of the most common behaviours. They often occur in clusters rather than as individual actions:

arrogance, manipulation, cruelty, sneakiness

misusing banter deliberately, gaslighting, hypocrisy, lying, ignoring dishonesty, malicious gossip

prejudice, discrimination, blaming others

hubris, jealousy, envy

pessimism, competitiveness

revenge, fear, anger, passive-aggressive actions

insincerity

stubbornness

laziness

bullying and harassment

fraud, corruption

wilful blindness

agnotology, suppression

plagiarism.

> *Well, I don't like her and never have. Who does she think she is? Coming here with all her degrees and experience. I am just not going to be helpful.*

❧⚜❦

> *I really don't know why he does not find it funny when we call to him, 'Slowly, slowly.' He walks weirdly and sometimes must use a walking stick. As a joke, I asked Saira to stare at him. He has gotten upset—what an immature person.*

REFLECTION

Consider your current experience with toxic behaviours at work and complete the table below.

List the behaviours that you are currently experiencing.
Who is using these behaviours and when?

Usually, the people who use these behaviours know they will cause distress. Occasionally, someone who is not toxic will use one of these actions because they are tired or not thinking clearly.

Having realised the error of their ways, the person will admit fault, apologise, and put things right.

Each of these toxic behaviours or related actions affect the targeted person. When considering their impact, we take into account the frequency, severity and intensity of the behaviours. In cases of toxicity, it is vital to look at the effect of the behaviour on the person. Being shouted at once a month in public can be as demoralising as being threatened with non-renewal of a contract once a week or being the continual subject of gossip or banter.

Consider the questions below.

What is the effect of the behaviours you have been experiencing on your...?

Thinking and decision-making

Minimal negative impact   Overwhelming

◄─────────────────────────────────►

Ability to concentrate

Cannot focus   Can concentrate

◄─────────────────────────────────►

Making mistakes

Too many   Very few

◄─────────────────────────────────►

Anticipation of the next negative comment or behaviour

Always alert   Calm and prepared

←——————————————————————————→

Stress levels

Calm and centred   Very stressed

←——————————————————————————→

Work social life

Isolation from colleagues   Good relationships

←——————————————————————————→

Private life

Negative impact   No impact

←——————————————————————————→

Emotions

Negative impact   No impact

←——————————————————————————→

Patience

Negative impact   No impact

←——————————————————————————→

Please summarise what you have learned about yourself.

WHY DO PEOPLE USE THESE BEHAVIOURS?

The flippant answer is 'because they can.' The culture can permit such actions, and it may well be that leadership expects, tolerates, or ignores them.

Some people are very insecure and want to control others or gain power through intimidation and other negative actions, such as revenge and cowardice. Some perpetrators were subject to these behaviours themselves and now repeat them. Others may not know any better and have normalised these actions as 'this is how you manage people.'

There is a lot of literature on how there are psychopaths, sociopaths, narcissists, or Machiavellians at work; people with these characteristics are also prone to using shadow behaviours. However, they are often undiagnosed in the business world.

It can help to understand why someone has negative behaviours, but we should not then use that as an excuse or justification for the person's deeds. A person's history can explain their actions, but we all have a choice we can make – to repeat history or not.

People who use these actions find it difficult to change, especially if leadership does not address their deeds. Organisations usually ignore such behaviours, so the perpetrator gets very little consequences and requests to change. Some may not want to change, or they lack any external motivation to do so. Alternately, a few like having power and ability to control and manipulate others, so they continue regardless of the damage caused. Most will consider themselves to be decent people.

> *I honestly don't believe my manager, who has said that I must stop intimidating staff. Does she not realise that these people need to be kept under control, as my best boss used to?*

The actions described above affect many people, not just the targeted ones. Witnesses are also affected, especially if they feel unable to act on behalf of the targeted individual.

SIGNS THAT YOU ARE WORKING IN A TOXIC ENVIRONMENT

Below are the typical signs; which ones apply to you?

Unhealthy communication

Poor or awful leadership

Ineffective HR systems

Ineffective internal justice

Cliques

Negative gossip and banter

Frequent use of toxic behaviours

An 'atmosphere' of intimidation

Lack of loyalty and motivation

Very little compassion, respect or decency shown

Having favourites

Serial failure to tackle toxicity

People just doing their jobs and little more

High use of sick leave

A lot of staff turnover

Staff feel very limited

REFLECTION

The signs of toxicity in my organisation are:

The positive aspects of my organisation are:

(Positives are worth listing if they exist, even if few people use them.)

Hopefully, you now have a greater understanding of the toxicity that is present in your work. Let's move on to tackling it and finding a healthier way to cope.

GATHERING YOUR STRENGTHS

THE WONDERFUL YOU

When you are the target of toxicity and awful behaviours, you can feel cut off, 'less than,' diminished, and demoralised. Worse still, a part of you may believe what is being said about you, even if you know objectively that it is not true.

Perpetrators are good psychologists and know who to target. They seek vulnerability. They rarely choose people who are very confident.

Being vulnerable is not a fault, except in some business settings, when it is called a weakness. Especially those in which projecting an image of being 'super strong' or invincible is valued. This is common in very competitive environments where it is OK to disregard others for the sake of winning or promotion.

REFLECTION

Let's stop and think about your many brilliant qualities.

How do they reveal themselves at work?

What qualifications and expertise led to you being appointed in this job?

If you were in a supportive environment, how good could you be at your job?

What do you consider is your greatest achievement at work?

How brave have you had to be at your work?

Having pondered these questions, please write a paragraph that affirms the brilliance of you.

I am great at what I can do. I am talented, knowledgeable, and kind.

SELF-CARE

We can forget to look after our well-being, mental health, and physical health when we are in a negative environment. This can lead to us being unable to cope as well as we should. For example, not eating lunch because a bully in the staff cafeteria loudly asked if you had put on a lot of weight could lead to you feeling weak during the day, and therefore functioning below par.

Good self-care includes having effective habits in these areas:

>Well-being–looking after your body by exercising, healthy eating, staying hydrated, and sleeping well

>Making sure that you respect yourself, build and develop your self-esteem and self-confidence

>Financial matters and resources–making sure that you are managing your money well, looking after the material goods you have, living within your means, and contributing to sustainability

>Relationships–ensuring that the people in your work and life are mutually beneficial and supportive

>Career–that you are working towards your career goals in a realistic and healthy way

Hopes and dreams—having 'creative stretch,' recognising your potential, and building hopes and dreams that are the most positive and realistic way forward for you

It is vital that you have regular physical and mental health checks to make sure you are healthy and prioritise any health needs and treatments you have.

Our bodies, minds, and emotions are fallible, and it is important that we look after them, especially when very stressed. This is when we can forget self-care.

REFLECTION

Think about your own work and home life.

What have been your self-care routines and habits in the following areas?

Well-being

Increasing self-respect and self-confidence

Financial matters and resources

Relationships

Career

Hopes and dreams

Physical health

Mental health

HOW HAVE YOU COPED?

How you have managed in your work environment will depend on the strength you feel, the power you have, and the courage you possess to act. You can use the human resource and internal justice systems if they are present and functional. Some people seek help from these systems and are successful. Others access them, experience retaliation, and continue to suffer. In some organisations, people know that there is no point in saying anything, so they just carry on for as long as possible, or they leave. Here are some questions. Which is your current approach?

Have you complained? What has happened? How hopeful are you about a resolution?

Do you want to resign? What actions have you taken to look for somewhere else to work?

Will you stay and just cope? If so, at what cost to you and your relationships? Who helps you? What steps have you taken to protect yourself? — e.g., being extra nice to your domineering manager so that they don't lose their temper with you, allowing your manager to give you extra work even though you are overloaded.

If you have engaged with toxicity through either preemptive or reactive behaviours, what impact has it had on your self-esteem and confidence?

How have you coped? To what extent is there a way forward in this company?

What boundaries will you set about what you will accept, and what you will confront and how, in the future?

I keep coming to work because I must. I have taken so much sick leave, and my annual appraisal was bad. Why aren't they listening to me when I say that Simon is making my life so hard? Why am I even asking? Simon is awful and knows he can do what he wants because he is best mates with the chief executive.

✺

I just lie low. Speaking up made things worse.

✺

I have had enough; I've made an appointment to see the director without my managers knowing.

CONSIDERING YOUR OPTIONS

Here are some suggestions and steps to take. Please select or alter the ones that match you.

LETTING GO OF THE PAST

When we experience negativity, we carry it with us in our memories, bodies, and emotions. These influence us in the present, e.g., we may be hypervigilant to daily cues that, while ordinary, could trigger a negative memory.

> *Mary's manager kept belittling her every chance she found. Mary was the subject of a lot of negative banter. Her manager liked to wear green; Mary became hypersensitive whenever she spoke to someone who was wearing green.*

There are various ways to let go of past events.

1. Find a quiet place and time. Have two chairs in the room. Sit in one and make yourself comfortable. Imagine that the toxic individual is in the other chair. What would you like to say to them to address their behaviour? Having 'had' that conversation, find a way of saying goodbye to that memory. What have you learned? What could you do differently next time? Which emotions do you need to let go?

    If it is impossible to have the imaginary conversation, you could write a letter to the toxic person. Read the letter and then destroy it. Then answer the above questions.

2. Find somewhere to sit with a table in front of you. Think of all the negativity that has happened to you. Put out your hands with the palms uppermost. 'Place' every negative experience in your hands. Then close and dust your hands, removing and destroying the negativity; 'wash your hands' of it. Then think of all your positives and strengths and imagine filling your hands with them. Now place the positives in a pocket so you can take them out whenever you want.

3. Sometimes it can help to seek support from a mental health professional such as a clinical psychologist or counsellor.

PAUSING FOR A MOMENT

These exercises will help you reflect.

Stop and have a look at your responses and reflections throughout this pocketbook. What do they say about your strengths, motivation, and courage to address the situation you are in? What is the image that comes to mind?

How would you feel if you became braver? What support do you need? Again, what is the image that comes to mind?

Imagine that you are standing in the middle of your organisation, surrounded by the positive and the negative. You have your current image as your protection.

Now imagine that it is the future and create your future self. Imagine you are walking with your future self as protection. Step into your organisation. How do you feel?

If you were to become your future self now, what help, and support would you need? What habits and behaviours could you adopt? Who could help you? What cues could you have in your daily life to remind you to change.

Now, stop and think about whether you are ready to change. If you are, then please have a look at our suggestions below. If you are not, then that is fine. You know yourself best. Please remember that strengths come in many shapes and forms, from speaking up to being silent. Whichever option you choose, please make sure that you develop and maintain a good self-care plan. Above all, think about how you could protect yourself and make yourself appear less vulnerable.

What self-affirmation could you create to remind you of your excellence and ability to cope? Remember to create one based on your values. Make it realistic. "I am decent, honest and capable." "I am working on my self-confidence."

TAKING FORMAL ACTION

In some situations, the best (and possibly the only) option you have is to take more formal action.

To do this, you will need courage, realism, and excellent support. Without these, acting can be difficult and daunting.

It is helpful to take a structured and stepped approach. Start with an objective assessment of what has happened. Make sure that you have kept an accurate record, with evidence, of what you have experienced.

Find out the processes for reporting and internal justice. Try to determine what the politics are for speaking up. Is the leadership in favour and willing to listen, or are they just paying lip service?

If you decide to go ahead, then build your case so that it is logical and objective. Describe what happened and the impact it had on you. Don't provide opinions, e.g., 'He does this because he is a bully.' Instead, provide facts, such as, 'These are the statements that William has made to me in writing and in public.'

Once you are sure, discuss your case with a trusted friend or colleague. Seek legal advice and the views of the staff representative if these are present and available.

When you are ready, use the agreed routes for seeking internal justice, e.g., Ombuds services, ethics offices.

You may need to ask for protection from the individuals who are targeting you. Remember that they are likely to have allies from whom you may also need protection.

As you progress in your case, try to prepare yourself for all the potential roadblocks and hurdles. Know that a quick resolution is unlikely. On average, it takes over eighteen months for a solution to be reached.

If they reach a solution, make sure that it is one that satisfies you in your life circumstances.

> *Ardal's new manager falsely accused her of inappropriate behaviour at a conference, without specifying what she had done. Ardal was told that there was firm evidence of gross misconduct (sackable offence) and then placed on leave without pay. After a letter from her lawyer, her organisation finally admitted that the behaviours of concern were 1. Popping conference balloons,*

> *and 2. Arriving 15 minutes early to the conference dinner!*
>
> *Although the organisation knew Ardal had legal representation, the solution they offered was that she could return to work if she admitted fault. They would then place a note in her HR file for six months. Ardal agreed, as her family needed her income to survive.*

Sometimes, even when a person proves their case, they can experience retaliation. Fortunately, most organisations have policies to protect whistle-blowers which, however, do not always work as they should.

It is positive that, occasionally, there is a good resolution when someone speaks up.

> *The last team Kyle managed finally had the courage to report her for her continuous harassment and misuse of funds. This had been going on for years. Fortunately, the national leadership listened and instigated an investigation. They exonerated the team, and they let Kyle go.*

One effect of speaking up is that it helps others feel brave. Consider the impact of the #MeToo and #BlackLivesMatter movements. The world is different with so many voices speaking. This helps those who previously had been silent and just endured and suffered.

LESS FORMAL ACTION

Another, less formal way of speaking up is to elect to talk to the person directly. This can be difficult, as the perpetrator will not expect it. Make sure you have built a logical and clear description of the behaviours of concern. Prepare for the meeting, perhaps rehearse what you want to say with a trusted person. Try to ensure that the person you want to talk to is in a place and time where they feel comfortable. Choose only one or two issues at a time. Focus on behaviours and not opinion. Start by praising the person. Ask for a good mutual solution. Say that you want to work with the person for the wider organisational purpose—doing so reminds both of you that the aim is to produce a resolution for the higher intention. Then discuss the key behaviours in turn, ask for an explanation and a way forward. Hopefully, this will work. If it does not, then think about what happened and what may occur next. What actions may you need to take to resolve the issues while making sure you are safe?

Alternatively, you could alter your approach. For example, if there is a colleague who keeps passing on her work to you, challenge her diplomatically rather than simply accepting the tasks. You could say, 'Thank you for considering me. Please let me know how our manager will respond if I take over.' This could work, especially if the person has not informed the manager that they are giving you their work. We cannot change another's behaviour, but we can shape them by how we respond to them.

BUILDING YOUR CONFIDENCE

All the above suggestions require a good amount of confidence. Consider how you can build your confidence. Perhaps carry an image of someone or something that reminds you of the poise you want. What would a confident person wear and say? What would be their posture?

Adopt these postures and words even when you are not confident. Remember to interact positively with people so that you are both listening and engaging. Avoid speaking too quietly or too loudly.

STAYING SILENT SOMETIMES OR ALWAYS

Sometimes, you may feel you have no other option than to remain working within a toxic environment and be silent. You may feel it is the safest thing to do, or the pragmatic thing to do in the short term, hoping things will improve. Sometimes, we normalise awful behaviour as a way of coping. People stay for financial reasons or because of what they have already invested in the job.

> *I really don't know why I have put up with this for so long. There are days when I almost don't mind what they do and say to me. This job is near home and convenient for me. I am available anytime for Dad, who lives near me. He needs me. Seeing the GP's counsellor has helped.*

It is not always a straightforward decision. But it is important to stay in touch with the reasons you are staying, and to recognise that there are risks involved in staying and saying nothing–risks to your health and your own behaviour and expectations. Your sense of what is acceptable behaviour may become skewed, and you can forget what being decent is. You may start believing the awful things you hear; this could lead to your self-esteem decreasing, and you could become depressed.

Being quiet and staying where you are for a short or long time means that you are suppressing yourself and using a lot of energy, depleting your energy reserves. It is important to find a way of maintaining your self-respect and boundaries. Make sure that you are looking after your well-being, that you have dreams and hopes, that you continue to recognise what the situation is in your workplace, and that you surround yourself with caring people beyond it. Try not to pick up any habits or ways of those who are toxic; do not be 'infected' by their behaviour. Focus on your own positive attributes.

Be careful of becoming too stressed which may lead you into self-sabotage. This may make the situation worse even if that is not your intention. For example, not completing a project as agreed, even though you have time, knowing that this will annoy your boss who is harassing you.

If someone is trying to goad you, then remain calm. This may involve ignoring the person or walking away. If you show your vulnerability, then this is likely to incite the perpetrator to further action. It may be necessary to behave as though you are unaffected to get through the day. Remember that you are unlikely to be the only person suffering like this.

Remember that you can isolate aggression and bad or antisocial behaviour by surrounding the person with kindness and good behaviour. It is hard for people to continue to be aggressive when others are calm and considerate. Your own positive behaviour can be a personal force, but also a beacon for others.

Don't share too much personal information in work conversations. Maintain your privacy.

Always know and remember your own self-worth. You are a valuable member at work, with much to contribute to life.

LEAVING THE ORGANISATION

People leave toxic situations. This is completely understandable. But it is vital that the person leaves on their own terms. That they go to a new job or vocation should be of their choosing, not because it was the only option available.

If this is your situation, stop and think about what you would like as your next career move. What is your dream in terms of work? Then work out how you can achieve your dreams.

If you are worried about references, then remember that you can always take steps to protect yourself to avoid being given a bad reference. For example, ask your manager's manager or HR for a reference, if your boss has been the toxic one.

When you leave, prepare for some sabotage and game-playing.

> *Sudinda was finally moving to a better organisation, after having been there doing his best for ten years. Most staff, except the two perpetrators (his managers), valued his contributions. Interestingly, the managers could not organise a leaving do for him. Supposedly, there was an administrative error.*

RECOVERY

Please know that there will probably be a point when the toxicity will end, at which point you can recover and realise how much it has affected you. Take steps to learn and remember your own self-worth—that you are the person you see in the mirror, not what toxic people's behaviour implies.

MY PROMISE
TO MYSELF

Pause and think about what you have read here. What have you remembered? What will you do now?

Therefore, what is the promise you will keep in the coming months? And who will support you?

My promise is ....

....

My supporters are ....

Thank you. Please contact us if you have questions.
www.healthyleadership.world
Instagram: healthyleadership.world

REFERENCES

These are available on our website:
www.healthyleadership.world

Printed in Great Britain
by Amazon